# GRIEF AND COMEBACK

## LAURA BIDDLE

"Blessed are those who mourn, for they shall be comforted."

*Matthew 5:4*

# CONTENTS

# Introduction

Dear Reader,

Thank you for trusting me with the gift of healing broken hearts and soothing anguished souls. Crafting these monthly columns for the *Newburyport Daily News* about grief and comeback has been a wonderful way to connect with you. I have treasured every interaction and every moment reflected in these essays.

This book is meant to acknowledge angst and calm sorrows caused by grief. My intention is to offer stories and blessings that help rekindle relationships and remind us that love never dies. Each chapter is designed to recognize a kind of loss, to affirm the difficult emotions that emerge from that experience, and to inspire a way to come back to life and find joy.

Through this book, I want to open a dialogue with you about grief. I want you to know that your feelings matter and that you can heal while being true to yourself. Hopefully, my words are an invitation for you to rekindle your inner light and to know that you are not alone.

I am grateful that you and I are on this journey together.

*Sincerely,*
*Laura*

# 1
# Coming Home

A massage therapist and friend of mine called me with a suggestion: "Why don't you write a regular column for the *Daily News* about grief. So many people in this community are struggling with some kind of loss, and they don't know what to do with their feelings. As a grief counselor, you could offer some comfort through a regular article in the paper."

Curiously, I was listening to National Public Radio at the time. Tom Ashbrook, the host of *On Point*, who recently lost his wife, had just returned to work after a period of grieving. His program was titled "Grief and Comeback." He said, "One thing we know about life that is terrible and true: it ends. We don't get a choice about that. And sooner or later, that end comes to people that we love. And then, we grieve. In the past two months, that's been my path. A much-loved partner, lost. And plenty of grief. But for all the personal pain of it, grieving is an utterly universal experience. It comes to us all, essentially, at some point, over a parent, a lover, a friend, a child. It is one of the most human experiences. We are looking for some wisdom in this hour on how to make it through. And live again."

What I hope to do with this regular column in the *Daily News*, is to share stories and offer some comfort and healing. Together, I hope we'll discover ways to "make it through and live again."

Grief is one of the most common human experiences and one of the hardest to navigate. Grief can feel as painful as a physical wound, and have as much power to affect our daily routines as a form of paralysis. When grief has a grip, we feel like we are moving in slow motion, while the rest of the world is speeding ahead.

Death is one cause for grief, but not the only one. We grieve when there is a separation or divorce; when our children leave for kindergarten or college; when we are forced to depart from a job or a community; when our home is an unsafe place to live; when we are betrayed; when a beloved animal dies; when we receive a difficult diagnosis about our health; when violence destroys our sense of safety; and when power is misused at our expense. No matter how we get to the place of grieving, grief needs tending. Without attention, the emotions that emerge can be debilitating and can impact our future health and the significant relationships in our lives.

The first step in healing grief and coming back to life is awareness and acceptance. Rather than telling ourselves to "get over it" or that "other people have it much worse." or "its been long enough, time to move on," healing and comeback require being gentle with our selves. There is no correct time frame for grieving and no proper way to feel.

What you feel matters. How you feel, whether it is numbness, fear, guilt, regret, relief, anger, sadness, or absolutely nothing, matters. YOU matter. To ignore or dismiss grief is to deny your humanity. Grieving makes us feel vulnerable, and we are a culture that resists vulnerability with passion. But coming back to life requires a willingness to be vulnerable, with ourselves first, and then with the people we love. So join me in the work of "grief and comeback."

As we begin this journey in this public forum, I invite you to take time to be gentle with yourself and to notice your grief. Have you lost something or someone important, recently or even long ago, and are you afraid to feel what you really feel? Perhaps reading this column will open up an opportunity for you to comeback home to yourself.

In closing, I offer an exercise that might be helpful. Take one small piece of paper and a pen and write down a loss. It doesn't have to be a big one - or even a recent one. Name the person or the situation and underneath the loss, write one feeling that has a grip on your heart. Just one.

Then say this blessing:

Here I am, just as I am. This feeling has a grip. As I name it and release it, may I be blessed and comforted. And may I live again. Bless also, the one who has died, that they may be at peace.

# 2
# Spiritual Healing After a Suicide

Leading a bereavement support group, I learned that several people in our group were grieving a suicide. When a loved one takes their own life, our grief is profound and deeply complex. And too often, what we feel is buried in a silent world of shame and confusion that sets us apart from each other when what we need most is connection. I hope today's column about grief opens up opportunities for you to make healing connections.

Spiritual healing after suicide is vitally important for bereaved family, friends and communities. Spiritual healing allows people to accept the truth and delve into the depths of despair while trusting in a promise that light eventually emerges out of the darkness. This light is *hope*. Feeling hopeful in our most difficult times is a spiritual practice. Most people who are grieving want to hold onto the hope that the person who has died is at peace, that the relationship didn't die, and that love lives forever, even after suicide.

A few years ago, my close friend from childhood took his life. I learned of his death while I was on sabbatical from my church. One evening, while waiting in a long line to get aboard the oldest trolley car in San Francisco, I saw my friend Steve walking along the street. I called out to him but he never turned. I knew for sure it was Steve because of his unique style of dressing: big work boots left untied, a bandana around his head, his sculpted face pointed straight ahead, and his swagger that always let me know how confident he felt. When he didn't respond to my voice, I decided to get in touch with him as soon as I returned to Massachusetts, if for no other reason than to ask him why he was visiting San Francisco and why he hadn't let me know. When I returned home two days later, I received a call from Steve's father.

"Laura, I am calling with hard news..... We need your help. Steve died. We thought you would be the best person to officiate at his funeral."

Shocked that I was hearing this news, I pulled over to the side of the road and asked the obvious question, "How did he die?" There was a long pause. I could hear him struggling through his tears. I knew something was terribly wrong. "He took his own life." After my shock and confusion settled a little, we both cried on the phone. I agreed to visit with the family the following day.

Later, I remembered my semi-encounter with Steve in San Francisco. I wondered whether my experience was a sign that he was spiritually present and was inviting me to help his family through this difficult time. *I share this only to illustrate that my trust in the power of spiritual connections deepened that day.*

A week later, the celebration of life for my friend Steve was packed with family and friends. We incorporated the truth of his suicide during the opening welcome. Relief and sorrow were evident in every eye of the congregation. At that moment, I realized how significant the truth can be in healing and prevention work around suicide.

When a loved one takes their life, there are many unanswered questions: *Why? What did I miss? How could I have prevented this? Does anyone understand?* There are questions about forgiveness: *Do you forgive me? Can I forgive myself? Can I forgive you? How can any of us forgive this?*

When someone we love dies in this way, we are starving to understand and to be understood. And in the spiritual realm of "I don't understand," there is the possibility that the relationship with our loved one can begin anew. Being open to that possibility helps us "comeback" and live again. An exercise that might open this conversation is letter writing. Write a letter to the one who has died expressing your honest feelings of confusion, sorrow, anger, and how much you miss them. Then let it BE. Set it aside. Stay open to your new relationship.

In closing, I offer this blessing: *Gentle and Forgiving Spirit, Bless our open and fragile hearts with your unending and unconditional love. Heal our brokenness. And bless the ones we love who have died.*

# 3
# Buried Grief

A young woman came to see me, crying uncontrollably. Her six month old cat had died of a heart attack and she couldn't stop the flow of tears. "I don't know if I will ever smile again." She said. "I can't go to work like this. I just can't stop crying."

After a few teary counseling sessions, during which she spoke about her love for animals and for this particular cat, I asked her a question. "Did someone you love die prior to this death?"

She hesitated between sobs and then answered, "Well, my Mom died when I was six years old. But that was 30 years ago."

Buried grief doesn't dissipate. Unattended grief doesn't go away. In fact, grief and all its manifestations, can be extremely patient, waiting in the depths of our souls for a moment to emerge. Sometimes, it is another loss that sets the grief free. And curiously, the "other" loss is often a beloved animal.

One of my friends once said to me, "Some animals come into our lives as spiritual guides. When their job is done, when the work of their relationship with us is complete, they are free to live or die in their own time and their own way."

Perhaps you have had the experience of losing an animal at a critical moment in your life. Maybe at the peak of a transition, or at a time when you thought your life was starting all over again. Have you ever cried so hard over the death of an animal that you thought you'd never smile again?

You may have been experiencing both the sadness of the immediate loss as well as the buried grief of another one. When unattended grief lies buried in our souls, it finds a time and a way to rise. Grief is one of those soul-friends we cannot ignore. When we experience a loss, the wounds we hold from previous losses can open up again and ooze everywhere.

Shortly after my divorce 21 years ago, my beautiful and loving dog became very sick and had to be put down. Leaving the Animal Hospital, I thought I'd never breathe again. In retrospect, I believe that my dog was a spiritual guide. He had come into my life before my marriage and he stayed with me to the end. When he died, I was in such a frantic mode of single-parenting, I hadn't wept for the loss of my marriage. His death gave me permission to weep.

An exercise that might help you understand whether or not you are re-experiencing grief is to remember a loss. Maybe your grief is the result of a broken heart, a geographical move, a betrayal, or a health crisis. Write one former loss down on a piece of paper. Then under the loss, list some of the feelings that gripped you at the time. Maybe uncontrollable crying was one of them. Maybe you felt numb. Did you feel anger, confusion, or a sense that you might never smile again? How did you cope with these feelings? Did you get busy? Did you weep a lot? Did you hide inside your home?

If grief has been buried and left unattended, you may discover that you are re- experiencing this grief every time there is a new loss in your life. If this is the case, then I offer a blessing for your journey: *Today, I welcome the familiar feeling of grief that has buried itself in my soul. By naming this feeling, I release it to the healing energy of hope. Bless me as I peel away the layers of grief and set my soul free. Help me love myself again. AMEN.*

# 4
# Fall Down Seven Times, Stand Up Eight

Hopelessness is a heavy feeling. Sometimes, after the initial shock and numbness of loss, there is a time of hopelessness, when grief has a grip and it's hard to envision something other than THIS sadness and despair. A man came to talk with me shortly after his wife of 25 years died of pancreatic cancer. His first question was about hope. "I feel completely devoid of hope. How do I find hope? I feel as if I'm stuck in a world without hope. Help me!"

Hope, I believe, begins with acceptance. To accept the moment that IS, is a spiritual practice. This loss, this feeling, this emptiness, this sorrow, THIS despair is real for now. Acceptance takes time and attentiveness; time that urges us to be compassionate with ourselves, trusting that hope will emerge through the multitude of emotions no matter how painful they may be. Acceptance is a practice of living NOW, with trust that this is a time for grief and there will be a time of hope. From here, there is only forward, and forward is hopeful. Acceptance is the first step in restoring hope.

One of the ways that I have learned to manage hopelessness is to find a purpose in the midst of grief. We have just watched the second Boston Marathon since the 2013 bombing. More than 30,000 runners entered the race with the purpose of restoring hope to survivors, family members, friends, Boston, and all people traumatized by that tragic day. As the runners finished, in spite of the wind and rain, many spoke about running to raise money for charities. All of the runners were holding out hope for people who are suffering from physical and emotional losses. Some of these losses were related to the marathon, but many of the charitable gifts from runners were for other types of losses such as a difficult diagnosis, domestic abuse, and brain injuries. Hope ran through the streets of Boston on April 20, 2015.

Hope was also the theme of a "Celebration of Life" service at Salem State University two weeks ago. When a student lost her life in a car accident, the community rallied to honor her with words, music, and dance. Woven into every aspect of the celebration of her life was the theme of hope which was sparked by a tattoo she wore on her arm, "Fall down seven times, stand up eight." She was a dance and education major and was familiar with falling down and standing back up. She knew the importance of accepting the "falls" in life while holding onto hope in the "stand-ups." For her friends and family this is her everlasting gift.

Hope in the face of loss emerges when we practice acceptance and find purpose. Hope rises after a period of grieving honestly; of feeling the emotional pain, no matter how excruciating. Hope looks very much like falling down seven times and standing up eight. Hope is living now with as much grace as you can muster. Hope is the lifeline you accept and the one you offer. Hope is compassion for yourself that you share with others.

Grief can be transformative, offering us a new lease on life with new purpose and new depth. In the midst of the pain and the sorrow of grief, we are invited to discover new truths about ourselves. Hopelessness can be transformed into hope. The journey begins with acceptance.

In closing, I offer this prayer: *O gentle and graceful spirit, I trust that you are a light in whatever darkness I bring to this moment. Help me open myself to hope, even as hopelessness has a grip. Grant me eyes to see the unending beauty of your creations, a heart softened enough to feel the everlasting presence of love, and a soul that can accept this loss and trust in the spirit of hopefulness.*

# 5
# Remembering With Gratitude

For some of us, growing older is tough. Aging in both body and mind is a perpetual reminder that nothing is permanent and that we are fragile human beings. Mirrors, for the aging-sensitive, become reminders of delicate skin and of days gone by. And they cause us to grieve because we see ourselves reflected back in one dimension.

But we are multi-dimensional. Aging can be both a source of grief and an opportunity to look in the mirror and feel exhilarated by the challenge to comeback to life with gratitude for all that has happened. Gratitude can be the antidote to the age-sensitive feelings of loneliness, fear, and uncertainty. Remembering with gratitude is a wonderful practice.

One of my friends has started a "remember journal." She, like so many of us, is extremely concerned about aging in mind and body. Recently, she saw the movie "Still Alice" based on the book by Lisa Genova. Her response to the story about a woman who is diagnosed with early Alzheimer's, was to exercise her mind regularly by *remembering*. Every day, she writes in her "remember journal" a story or a memory that inspires her heart and soul. Everyday, she comes back to life from the edge of grief by *remembering with gratitude*.

Remembering what WAS is a lovely way to grieve. Although most spiritual practitioners, including me, will encourage you to let go of the past, I believe that remembering stories and remembering people with love is a wonderful way to celebrate today.

Remembering is different than gripping or clinging. Remembering is different than dwelling in past mistakes or past obstacles. Remembering with gratitude is a way to find balance and celebrate what is happening now. With memories that stir your heart and soul shining through your eyes and face, the look of aging is simply a map of your life and your capacity to love along the way.

Remembering with love and compassion for ourselves can be a journey of joy and healthy aging. After my 82 year old father had a heart attack several years ago, he and his seven children thought it was time for him to stop being so active. We thought it was time for him to get rid of his Indian Motorcycle and focus more on painting and writing and tending to his beautiful garden. As a man of many hobbies, this seemed reasonable. However, after a year of taking-it-easy, Dad was bored. And he was starving to get back on his motorcycle and back into the land of adventure. He started writing about the trips we'd taken into Vermont and Maine. Weekly, he would call me with another memory that made his heart feel joy.

And then he made the bold decision to ride again. With a promise to be moderate in all things, he and I took a ride last summer to the Finger Lakes in New York state. And we have just returned from a week of riding in New Hampshire with my son Lee, wearing sweatshirts that say "Biddle Bikers — Three Generations." We will forever have this memory of riding together — oh so slowly and carefully.

These rides with Dad will end soon. Forever, I will remember with gratitude the times we laughed at stop lights, the ways he protected me during foul weather rides by hovering close behind, and the magnificent mountains and valleys that called to us each summer.

*Remembering with gratitude* makes aging look beautiful. When you look in the mirror today or tomorrow, bless your self with gratitude for all that has happened that lives in your heart and in your soul.

# 6
# Tragedy That Affects Us All

When a tragedy strikes, whether it is personal or distant, deep emotions of grief get triggered.

When nine Black people are murdered in their sanctuary, their safe haven, their spiritual home, anger, sadness, fear, and utter despair come rushing to the surface.

When 49 dancing, celebratory LGBTQ community members are massacred in their safe haven, shock slams our collective pulse and our heartbeats lose their rhythm.

When we are submerged in grief as a community, we realize that we are all connected in this vulnerable world. No one is immune from the grief of the loss at Emanuel African Methodist Episcopal Church in Charleston, South Carolina, or the loss at Pulse Nightclub in Orlando, Florida.

Sadness descended over the world on Wednesday night, June 17, 2015, and Sunday morning, June 12, 2016. Death hit us hard and fast. And there is nothing to do but weep together. We are a community grieving with each other.

Anger rises after someone has died. We long for a place or person into which our fury can go. We often rage at doctors who have been neglectful or have made mistakes. We take out our fury on family members and friends.

Anger caused by grief needs a place to go.

If we can't find an outside recipient, we turn anger on ourselves, letting guilt and regret consume our minds. Staying awake through the night, rehashing what we "should" have done or who we "could" have been, causes day-time irritation and moodiness. Anger caused by grief can be consuming.

Life gets dreary and sadder when anger has the final say.

On the Friday after the hate crimes at the Emanuel AME Church in Charleston, South Carolina, family members gathered to speak directly to the perpetrator of this horrific crime. Within two days of the murders, they had enough courage to look at the man who killed their loved ones and speak. "May God have mercy on you."

Forgiveness is an antidote to anger caused by grief. Not surface forgiveness but deep down authentic forgiveness. Not the kind of forgiveness that is based on obligation to God or to a religious institution. Coming back from grief, being free to move forward and speak clearly about the sadness and despair, includes forgiving ourselves and forgiving others.

I admit that if a family member of mine had been gunned down in their church, or in their nightclub sanctuary, my first reaction would not have been to forgive the shooter. And I am sure the act of forgiving on that first Friday after the racist attacks in Charleston was bitter and difficult. But I know that forgiveness is a way of healing after death.

Forgiveness, it's said, is the gift we give ourselves.

I believe that this is true. To hold fast to anger, to grip a grudge, to hate without relief, is sure to trap us in a life of sorrow and sadness. To forgive ourselves and others is a way to heal after loss.

I am not a proponent of pretend-forgiveness. In my view, we cannot forgive ourselves until we admit our guilt and regret, feel what these difficult emotions are doing to our bodies and souls, and let them go. And we cannot forgive others until we have explored the ways that we are torturing ourselves with self-blame and shame.

Coming back from grief happens when we forgive ourselves for whatever it is we "could'a, should'a, would'a" done. Seeing grief as our spiritual teacher enables us to have compassion towards ourselves and then towards another.

I do not feel compassion for the man who killed the nine worshipers in Charleston, or the one who killed 49 patrons of joy in Orlando. I am not suggesting that compassion for racist, homophobic murderers is a goal of grief and comeback. I do trust that forgiveness is born of compassion and compassion is born of grief. We are all in this situation together. These deaths have touched everyone.

As you proceed to process all that has happened and consider your losses with love for the people who have died, both far and near, be gentle with yourself. Have compassion for your anger, guilt, and despair. Choose forgiveness over vengeance. We make this world a better place when forgiveness has the final word.

# 7
# When Love Ends

"Love endures all things, hopes all things, believes all things."
*1 Corinthians 13:7*

Almost every wedding ceremony in which I have participated has included some or all of these words about love. For most people, seeking love, understanding love, and being loved is as important as anything. Love is the theme in life that consumes our hearts and souls. Feeling lovable in the eyes of another human being may be the most important feeling of all. Weddings and civil union ceremonies allow couples to stand before each other and proclaim their unending love that endures all things.

So, what happens to our hearts and souls when love doesn't last? What happens to our bodies when love doesn't endure all things; when we don't feel lovable or don't have the affirmation of love that hopes all things as our foundation? What happens? We grieve in heart, mind, body and soul. And this grief caused by lost-love, hurts as much as a body full of broken bones.

Relationships are tender living organisms. Love, though powerfully resilient, deeply passionate, and capable of navigating the rockiest of times, requires kindness, resilience, and attention. When relationships end, or when we take another person's love for granted, or when the tender gift of love is abused, grief and despair take hold.

Grief caused by a divorce or a break-up can be as physically painful as a body of broken bones. Every fiber of our being, after a loss such as this, feels as if it's on fire. And we become uber-sensitive to "normal" stuff: a kind word or a hug from a friend can launch a cascade of tears; a love story on film can stir up memories of lost dreams; a love song that once made us smile can grab hold of our heart strings with a fierce grip; a couple walking hand-in-hand can trigger an onslaught of sadness.

Grief from a break-up is compounded by its privacy. Unlike grief after someone has died, the grief caused by the ending of a relationship is an insidiously solo sorrow. Who wants to hear about or talk about unrequited love and loneliness all the time?

Further complicating the grief is living with the hopeful possibility that the ending was not the end. When someone dies, there is no doubt about whether the relationship could begin again. Death has a finality that leaves no room for hoping that the one who has died will reappear. But when a marriage or committed relationship ends, we are susceptible to remembering the relationship in only positive terms and hoping that *that* relationship might return, in the best possible way.

Few of us have been spared this kind of grief in our lifetimes. Pre-teens often think that their first love story is the one for all times. Teenagers can be completely derailed and changed by a break up. Twenty-somethings are prone to thinking that no one else will ever love them. In middle age, we can't imagine life without our partner.

"Coming back" from this type of grief requires self-love.

When I was singing with a local band here in Newburyport, we made a recording to benefit the Jeannie Geiger Crisis Center titled "Rising Up." One of the original songs was called "I Release You." The chorus still rings in my soul: "I release you and set my heart free, and I pray to God that my heart will again love me."

Coming back to life after the loss of a relationship is hard and painful, and it begins with letting go. Joseph Campbell once wrote: "We must be willing to let go of the life we've planned so as to have the life that is waiting for us."

I believe that every new spiritual journey begins with the ritual of letting go. Relationships are spiritual journeys. So if you are grieving the loss of a relationship, let go gracefully and be open to a new journey of love and possibility by loving yourself and trusting that you are a magnet for love that believes all things.

A blessing for your journey: *May love shine from deep within you. May your love of yourself attract the kind of love that honors and cherishes you. And may you trust that you are lovable.*

# 8
# Goodbye

Saying goodbye is wicked important. Last weekend, I stood in line with hundreds of parents who were saying "goodbye" to their first year college students. The youngsters were generally calm and excited. Grandparents, aunts, uncles and mostly moms and dads, seemed to be wearing the familiar mask of "fake it till you say goodbye then get in the car as quickly as possible before the tears won't stop."

My three children have all graduated from college as of this year. Their paths in and through higher education were unique to each of their learning styles and passions. What was common for me with each of my kids when I left them at college were the goodbyes. I felt like I was leaving them at kindergarten all over again; sending them off into a world that could be cruel and scary. My car rides home after every goodbye included sobbing, listening to music to stop my mind from wandering, and opening windows for the feel of fresh air in my face.

Maybe some of my readers recognize this ritual?

Saying goodbye is hard. Whether it's due to a re-location, a break-up, or a death, goodbye is one of the saddest words. When someone we love is dying, due to cancer, Alzheimer's, brain injury, old age, or any kind of disease that gives us a little time before death, saying goodbye is complicated. People tip toe around death and choose not to talk about real feelings or endings, because no one wants to admit the reality out loud. Speaking the truth makes it seem more real somehow. No one likes a goodbye.

But not speaking the truth creates the possibility that loved ones miss the opportunity to say "goodbye," which is a sacred gift.

Missing the opportunity can be devastating. When someone dies in a car accident, there is no goodbye. A suicide cuts off the chance to say this spiritual word. A plane crash robs us of this significant ritual.

Grief without a sacred ending, a warm and honest goodbye, hurts deeply.

On January 7, 2003, a 16 year old child from our community, Trista Zinck, was killed by a drunk driver. It was a snowy evening and Trista and her boyfriend Neil Bornstein were hit by a pickup truck. Neil suffered severe brain injury, while Trista had terminal injuries.

Early January 8, I was invited to join the Zinck family at the hospital. We surrounded Trista with love and prayers during her last hours of life. The conversations were heartfelt and sorrowful; and one-directional. Everyone hoped for a glimmer of consciousness from Trista so that we could experience the ritual of goodbye. But that opportunity never opened.

The funeral was packed with high school students and local community members who couldn't fathom the pain that the family was feeling. Many of the students at the service had never experienced death before. Trista's father Dave and mother Mary sat in the front row of the sanctuary and listened to the out pouring of love for their beloved daughter.

One of her friends from kindergarten was quoted saying, "I once asked Trista why she was always smiling. She told me life was too short to be unhappy."

Grieving a sudden death takes us to a terrifying place. A place in which anyone of us could find ourselves trapped. It is a place that can feel like we are falling into an abyss. Because grief after an accident, suicide, or terrorist attack robs us of the ritual of saying "goodbye."

How do we comeback from this kind of grief? I wish I had a magic wand to heal hearts torn apart in this horrific way. Without such a magical tool however, my response to this question is to create rituals, especially on significant days.

Holidays are wonderful times to light a candle at the family table and remember the one who was ripped away from your life. Remember her/him with stories that make you laugh and cry. And when you have shared a few of those wonderful memories, say "goodbye." Open an avenue for communication with this simple word and you may discover a new relationship emerges that allows you to heal.

Saying "goodbye" with sincerity is an important part of healing. Missing a chance to say "goodbye," because we are scared to admit the truth of an ending, could become a lifelong regret. So say it; say "goodbye." Let this word be an integral part of your daily routines, even if the one you love has already left.

Because in saying "goodbye" you begin a ritual that allows you to heal.

# 9
# Pregnancy, Loss, Grief

She did everything she could to protect herself from pregnancy. She used a diaphragm; he used a condom. With two layers of protection, she presumed that a conversation about what happens if she got pregnant was unnecessary.

And then it happened. All her good intentions were irrelevant. She was pregnant.

The timing was horrible. Just three weeks earlier, she had decided to end the relationship. His mean-spiritedness had turned into controlling behavior so she was planning a way to get out safely. Becoming pregnant was not in the plan.

Choosing abortion as a way to deal with her pregnancy was the hardest decision of her life. Choosing safety and sanity for her heart, mind, body and soul was a foreign concept. She had spent her adult life caring for others. Her future was devoted to a career of compassion and hope for the people around her. Choosing to terminate the pregnancy was not a political decision; it was a decision with life changing spiritual and emotional ramifications.

When she made the initial appointment at the clinic, she began to understand the mosaic of feelings associated with the procedure. In addition to being prepped for the physical experience, she was also warned about being heckled by protesters who would line the street outside the clinic. For weeks, the memory of hecklers, seemingly heartless, sent her sobbing alone to her bed at night, full of shame and humiliation.

Grief after an abortion is a silent and wickedly private journey. No one knows the depth of loss and sadness — the overwhelming sadness. No one knew when she was sitting in a lecture listening to discussions about women's rights to choose education and protect themselves from sexual assault, that she was aching inside; on the verge of tears at all times.

No one knows the depth of grief after an abortion, unless you've had one yourself.

Though mostly a solo journey, coming back from this silent sorrow can be softened by a partner. For some women, healing begins right away because someone in their life understands. Someone, a friend, a lover, a parent, a minister, a therapist, someone is willing to BE present to them without judgment or shame. When the agony of emotions are shared with one compassionate person, she knows that she is not totally alone in her path of healing and coming back to life.

But for many women, the silent sorrow that is born out of living with the stigma of abortion is grueling. The sight of a pregnant woman can trigger an avalanche of dark emotions. The word abortion, thrown into a conversation, can unleash a flow of tears that have to be stifled and suppressed. A friend or relative who is trying to become pregnant can unintentionally inspire deep sorrow.

One way that women slowly but surely comeback from this private grief is by remembering the date and honoring the experience. A simple acknowledgment of the day each year can help calm the feelings of loss. If there are regrets, this anniversary of remembering can be an annual opportunity to pay tribute to an experience that transformed the future and made life that much more precious.

Miscarriages are also sorrowfully quiet. Though not a choice, there is an inner grief that can affect everything about an outer life. Seeing other women, who carry a pregnancy to term, feeling happy and excited with anticipation, can become a trigger for sadness. Their joy feels like a reminder of the emptiness left behind a lost pregnancy.

Whether the ending is a choice or a miscarriage, the grief is very real and very hard. Being a kind friend and partner can make a huge difference in how a woman feels during this time. "Listening to understand" might be all that is necessary to accompany someone through their grief. Attentiveness to her sensitivity may be all she needs.

If you have experienced this type of loss, I offer this blessing: *May I be full of the spirit of loving kindness; may I be kind to myself; may I bless all that has transpired both within me and beyond; may my kindness be a blessing to others.*

# 10
# Hectic Holiday Season

Who hasn't dreaded the holidays at some point in their lives? Most people have had a year or more when they wanted to leap from mid-November to January as quickly and quietly as possible.

As a young single mom, I used to panic around this time of year. There were several layers to my uncomfortable feelings. The first was always about whether or not I had enough. Would I have enough gifts, enough food, enough joy, enough stuff for each child? Would one of them feel slighted because they didn't have *enough*.

The second consuming concern was being alone and feeling lonely. In the divorce agreement, my children were assigned by the courts to go to their other parent every other year, leaving me alone with my feelings and my empty home.

Expectations and community preparations around the holidays seemed to exacerbate my loneliness. Other people's happiness actually made me feel worse rather than better. I couldn't help but contrast my situation to all the joyful songs playing in every store, the light-hearted families walking through the malls, and the unending reminders of good-cheer on the radio.

I used to pray: Dear God, get me through these days so I can breathe again.

One year, one of my closest friends decided to sweep me away from my bi-annual despair. His thinking was that he could distract me from my sadness by exposing me to the joy of holiday cheer somewhere else in the world. God bless him for trying. But the feelings of grief lived within me, and nothing from the outside could "fix" that. Wherever I would go, I would bring my true self and all my memories, like it or not.

One of the ways that memories emerge in our minds is through our senses. I have a keen sense of smell. The fragrance of fires burning in a fireplace, for example, bring me back to my childhood before my parents were divorced. I remember the fires in the living room and, at least in my imagination, the joy that surrounded our Thanksgiving day rituals. There is one memory that will always make me laugh when I smell an outdoor fire on Thanksgiving. My mother had cooked an enormous turkey for her seven children and several guests. When the perfectly timed and prepared bird was ready, she placed it on top of the refrigerator to cool for a bit.

We had built a fire outside and everyone was gathered around it singing and playing guitars. Except our two Great Danes. They were inside with the bird. It turned out that the top of the refrigerator was not even a challenge for them. When we first realized that the turkey was half gone and spread all over the living room, there was some screaming and yelling in our happy scenario. But in the spirit of being grateful, we came up with a new meal-plan and re-grouped at the fire....

After a divorce, after a death, after a loss of any kind, the holidays are bitter sweet. Memories of good times can turn into broken hearts and lost dreams. For me, the smell of roasting turkey is another trigger for sorrow; the aroma of stuffing and butter-covered-bird recalls times of family gatherings and perceived joviality that can easily find a way to pull on my heart-strings.

Holiday memories can actually hurt so much when we are grieving that we don't want to participate in anything pertaining to being thankful or exchanging gifts. We don't want to put up lights or listen to music of the season. We don't want to be here!

"Coming back" to life during the holidays is a challenge to which you may not want to rise. The sadness you feel may be more honest and respectful of you and of the people who are absent from your life. *Pretending* that you are joyous can be exhausting and, quite frankly, damaging to your soul.

So how can we be honest and present to what is real right now, while the rest of the world seems to be so darn happy?

Create a new ritual for yourself and your loved ones. Rituals are the ground upon which we stand during festivals and celebrations. Rituals are what we remember when we have lost someone or something. Creating new rituals is a way to comeback while you are in the midst of grief.

One such ritual is as simple as lighting a candle to honor what has been lost. Whether the loss was natural and necessary, or a traumatic surprise, creating a new ritual can help usher in a sense of healing and hope. By sitting quietly near the light, with compassion for how you truly feel, you may discover a sense of peace and calm. Perhaps, in the quiet space between your darkness and the candle's light, you will feel a kind of gentle blessing.

My wish for our community and our world this holiday season is *peace* that surpasses our understanding. Keep your hearts and minds open to love that endures all things. God bless you.

# 11
# The Gift of Light

*"The people who walked in darkness have seen a great light.*
*Those who lived in darkness, on them light has shined." —Isaiah 9:2*

"Every year," said a friend, "my neighborhood would compete for who had the most beautiful light display. These were opulent homes, with large windows and extensive lawns. Competition during the summer months in the neighborhood was non-existent. Everyone mowed their own lawns and everyone offered to help mow the lawns of neighbors and friends.

But when December came around: "Game On!" One year, a living Santa was hired to sit on the front steps of one of the houses and welcome children from all over town. Bringing their gift lists to him, many children gathered on the colorfully lighted lawn, assisting with the annual *win*.

The games ended the year one of the neighbors lost a child. No one in the community felt as if they could "put on" a light display while their friends were suffering so badly. That was a number of years ago. We haven't seen lights in that neighborhood since then - at least not extravagant ones."

When friends and neighbors are grieving, most of us don't know how to respond. We have a tendency to tip-toe around other people's sorrow. We are afraid to inquire as to how people are *feeling* because they might just tell us the truth. And in the face of true feelings, what would we say to make everything better. We especially don't know what to say when holidays come around. We curtail our own joyous rituals out of fear that we might exacerbate their sadness or make them remember their loved one every time they step out of their home.

The truth is that when we are grieving the loss of a child, or any loss around this season of the year, we remember the ones who have died all the time, everywhere, forever and ever. Nothing anyone says or does causes us to remember a loved one. However, these months of long dark nights can amplify the loss, as can the ritual of giving and receiving gifts. These are the triggers that are difficult to navigate, especially when the loss is a child.

My recommendation for neighbors and friends of people who are grieving is the practice of *being* Light: Light that overcomes darkness, that feeds souls, that hopes all things, and that believes in love that never dies. This Light looks like comfort, sounds like listening, and feels like tender loving kindness. This Light is not talkative; it admits discomfort while trusting the gift of being present; and it has arms to offer a warm and loving embrace.

This Light can be a hug, a note that says "sending warm greetings," or a simple conversation that begins with "I have been thinking of your loved one this season." Naming the one who has died, with sincerity, is a way of honoring their life.

I am a firm believer in our human capacity to *be* Light. I believe that each time we step into the light, each time we allow light to wash over us as a healing force, we absorb the ability to carry that light for others. Even if we are grieving, being compassionate with ourselves makes room for Light to shine from deep within us. And that Light is all we need for our participation in healing conversations.

Being Light invites an awareness that light is insignificant without darkness. When our homes are filled with the brightness of daylight, we don't need to turn on lights. When we are walking on a sunny beach, we don't need to pull out a flashlight to guide our path. When a fresh layer of snow is reflecting the rays of the sun through our windows, we don't need to reach for a candle to illuminate the room.

Darkness invigorates our yearning for light.

Darkness provides the contrast necessary for light to shine brightly. Being *Light*, when you can't think of what to say or what to do, might be the best gift you can offer.

As we steer our way into the new year, perhaps trusting in our capacity to be and bring light into the darkness will usher in some comfort and peace for people we care about who are grieving. Trust that words are not always necessary for a healing conversation.

Blessings, my friends.

# 12
# Let It Be

*"When I find myself in times of trouble, mother Mary comes to me, speaking words of wisdom, let it be."*

*Paul McCartney, 1970*

His mother had died of cancer when he was fourteen. Like most teenagers who lose a parent, or someone they love, he probably wasn't prone to talking about her. Friends and relatives likely expected him to "move on, get over it, bounce back." He expected the same of himself. But her imprint was deeply embedded in his heart and soul.

Playing music, writing songs, and forming a band became his passion. He met John Lennon in 1957 when he was 15, only a year after his mother had died. Joining John's band was the beginning of a new chapter in his life. One of excitement and popularity, as well as grief. His mother never knew him as one of the Beatles.

When the band was closing the door on their magnificent and innovative relationships in 1968, Paul wrote a song titled "Let it Be." In the midst of the turmoil of the Beatles breaking up, Paul McCartney had a dream in which his mother Mary visited him. In interviews, he described the dream as an inspiration for the song. He said, "It was nice to visit with her again. I felt very blessed to have that dream."

Adding to his explanation of the meaning of the song, McCartney said that his mother Mary spoke to him, "It will be all right, just let it be."

Death of a parent or a beloved mentor can derail a child at any age. Teenagers are prone to thinking that death means the relationship is permanently over leaving no possibility for communicating or connecting. Even adults who have a deep faith in resurrection or a belief in an afterlife, can get derailed by the death of a parent, a mentor, or someone who plays an influential role in life.

"Let it be," said Mary in Paul's dream, more than a decade after her death. "It will be alright, just let it be."

People have told me, in the rawest moments of their grief, that they are desperate to have a "sign" from the one who has died. Hungry for something that opens a door to their presence and to a sense of their peace, human-grief calls out to the Universe: "I want a visit in a dream or in some other way. I pray every night that I will connect with my loved one. I hope that I might see a "sign" that lets me know everything is alright."

At these times, when our hearts and souls are yearning for connection, I like the words of the song: *"When I find myself in times of trouble, mother Mary comes to me. Speaking words of wisdom, let it be."*

Being open to signs of everlasting love can heal broken hearts and souls. Being open to a sign is a spiritual practice that is often accessed during sleep, when our bodies and minds are letting everything BE. Being open to "signs of eternal love" can happen in random places and situations.

A friend of mine, a mother of two children, whose husband died by suicide, recalls her son's observation the first month after his death. "I keep seeing eagles flying over me. I think it's Dad saying he is with us. Even at the cemetery, an eagle flew overhead."

A student at Salem State University lost her father suddenly last fall. His heart attack took him in the middle of the night leaving her no opportunity to say good-bye. The next day, as she was leaving her house to meet with family at the funeral home, she found pennies on the sidewalk. Picking up one after another, she felt as if her father was telling her something: "Penny for your thoughts. I love you." Ever since that day, she finds pennies in the most obscure places. For her they have become "signs" that her Dad is near and loving her always.

In a dream recently, a young father who lost his mom right before the birth of his son, had a visit from his former minister who died on the same night as the dream. In the dream, the minister was smiling as he asked: "How are you coming home?" The young man woke from his sleep with a sense that this minister had created a bridge for his mom who was waiting to come home to their relationship. The dream was a sign that a visit was coming.

"Signs" of everlasting love are comforting when we are grieving. Perhaps you have encountered a sign or experienced a visit from someone who has died. Maybe you know the feeling of peace that surpasses our understanding because you have connected with a loved one after death. Or you might be someone who longs for such a connection. I have found that adapting the words from Paul McCartney's song as a prayer can help us be open to whatever signs might be coming:

*When I find myself in times of trouble, please come to me. Speaking words of wisdom, help me **let it be.***

# 13
# "Being" Is Purpose Enough

A recent college graduate decided to join the Peace Corps. He was an activist at his school. Advocating for social justice and speaking out on behalf of women's rights, he was motivated by movements of compassion and change. The Peace Corps seemed to be the perfect place to begin his work in the world.

Assigned to a rural village in another country, he packed his bags with the good intentions of making a big difference.

Upon his arrival at his new home, he was told with absolute clarity, YOU CAN DO NOTHING FOR SIX MONTHS. This rule was hammered home several times before he boarded a bus and was driven into the wilderness of another world.

Doing nothing in the face of suffering and poverty is really difficult for an activist. Doing nothing except listening and learning from other people's lives and experiences is not easy when your energy is urging you to move mountains. Doing nothing but hearing the truth of other people's stories is simply hard for a mover of movements.

After the six months of *being* rather than *doing*, he was instructed to gather the folks he had met along the way into a "town-meeting." This turned into a circle of compassionate conversations about what was most important for the community moving forward.

The Peace Corps guy wanted to replace the roof on the school. After six months of watching it slowly collapse while students were learning, he knew that repairing the roof was the best use of his activism.

But the villagers wanted something very different. They wanted a fence to be built around their cemetery. They wanted to honor their loved ones who had died with a well crafted, beautiful, protective wall. So Peace-Corps-guy used his organizing skills and resources to build a fence around the cemetery. By the time he and the villagers were finished, he had heard stories about the people who were buried in the cemetery and he had developed a deep appreciation for the grief of the community.

Honoring the people in our lives who have died might be the most important thing we can do together. Respecting the fact that our friends and neighbors who have lost someone they love, may simply want to spend their money and time remembering them, could be the most sacred gift we can offer. Creating places and spaces that protect memories and foster connections is a profoundly intimate way to grieve together and to allow relationships to grow after a death.

Sometimes, when someone dies, doing nothing for six months is the best way to begin grieving.

- Listening to our heart's sorrows is enough.
- Hearing the music that keeps the relationship alive is sufficient.
- Smelling the clothing of the person we love is healing.
- Touching the chair where they sat every night is comforting.

Coming back from loss, healing through grief, has no proper timeframe. Pondering what is the best way to honor the person who has died may take time. During this time, you may want to listen to the voice of your soul that suggests how you want to honor your relationship and the person you love.

When Peace-Corps-guy finished building the fence and listening to the stories attached to the many lives buried in the cemetery, he asked what else he could do to help the villagers.

"We need a new roof on our school."

Giving ourselves permission to do nothing after a loss is harder than it seems. Whether we are grieving retirement from a career, unemployment, death, or relocation, doing *nothing* feels counter-productive in a busy world. But, this spiritual practice may create room for new possibilities and open a channel for building beautiful memories that look like something beyond our comprehension.

Perhaps your heart and soul are yearning to know what to do right now as you think about what you have lost in this last year. This is a good season to practice doing nothing as a way to allow yourself to grieve.

Eventually, you will build the roof that needs to be built. Don't worry!

# 14
# Finding Home

Dear readers,

Thank you for a year of dialogue and depth. Authoring this column has allowed me to connect with you in personal ways that I treasure. Your support has encouraged me to continue writing for the *Daily News*.

In response to the good grief work that we are doing, a friend recently sent me this article. I think it adds a wonderful personal touch to our conversation. Enjoy this essay by Clark Webb.

\* \* \*

June 3, 2014 — A cancerous tumor was located on my mother's pancreas today.

July 15, 2014 — They were supposed to remove the cancer today. That did not happen. It is Stage IV.

November 23, 2014 — My mother passed away today. It has not even been six months.

March 4, 2015 — I became a father today.

January 9, 2016 — I had a dream today that would change everything. I was asked by a man, "How are you getting home?" and I think I finally have an answer.

This span of twenty months was an emotional roller coaster to say the least. To say I felt lost before, during and after two major life events, within three months of each other, is an understatement.

Diagnosis of cancer, finding out my wife was pregnant, witnessing my mother's battle, watching my mother take her last breath, becoming a father....it was almost too much and it nearly broke me. Well, actually, it did break me.

I was like Humpty Dumpty sitting on the wall; a fictional character created by, not mine, but others' opinions, desires, beliefs & failures. Then, one summer day, a nasty wind kicked up and blew me off of that wall and I fell and fell hard. I was shattered, but in such utter shock that I laid there in pieces, for quite some time, still thinking I was sitting on the wall.

Slowly, however, I began to realize I was not myself. I tried to reassemble, but my body and mind were too disjointed; nothing matched. Parts of me were anger while other shattered pieces were grief; shards of me were fear while others were ecstatic joy. With guidance and time, though, the many parts of me began to mingle and meld and I was slowly able to put myself back together again; maybe not completely, but at least enough to stand and brush myself off.

On my feet again I realized two things: I was somehow a better version of my former self, although a work still in progress, and if I was ever going to find home, whatever that meant, falling and being broken was necessary. One can only do so much while sitting on a wall, watching the world go by.

So began my journey, but, still a bit dazed and confused, I had no idea where I was supposed to go or where I belonged. The concept of "home" kept driving me forward, but it was more of a mirage than anything. I tried talking to my mother, hoping for guidance, but I couldn't hear her. I would go to sleep hoping she would point the way in a dream or, at least, show up so we could talk openly and honestly for once allowing me closure. That never happened, but someone else did.

I mentioned earlier a dream that would change everything. I do not dream often or vividly, or even remember details past an hour upon waking, but this dream will forever be with me and it goes something like this:

I am in my hometown and am in a hospital. I walk into a room and see a close childhood friend sitting next to a man in a bed. The man in the bed smiles at me as I walk through the door and says it is great to see me. I respond that I am so happy to see that he is awake since, last I heard, he was in a coma. He then asks me, "How are you getting home?" to which I respond, "I don't know." He smiles his infectious smile, pats my friend on the leg and says, "Don't worry, my son will take you." And then I wake from the dream...

The man in my dream was my parents' pastor, a close family friend and someone I had known since I was eight years old. Not even a year after my mother's passing, he was diagnosed with melanoma and when I went to sleep on June 9th, 2016 he was, sadly enough, in a coma and at the tail end of his battle with cancer. When I woke from this dream, I found out he had passed only hours earlier.

I believe this man visited me to act as a bridge between my mother and I. Afterwards, it was as if a conduit had been opened because I began to see that my mother was listening and helping me to figure out where home was and where my family of three belonged. Buying a home became a reality within a week of that dream. A desperately needed career change became a strong probability only days later.

The true lesson learned, however, is that "home" is so much more than four walls or the perfect job. In terms of grief work, "home" is knowing that those that have passed on are still with us, guiding us when we are lost and holding us when we are missing them. They can be seen in every smile and tear and can be heard in the laughter of a child.

My son will never have the chance to meet his grandmother, but when he is playing by himself, laughing and talking to nobody, I know that my mother is beside him. That, my friends, is finding home.

# 15
# Practicing Sensitivity

"Will you people stop talking about your 'perfect' family!"

"*Please*, don't send a joyous holiday card during the first year of my grief."

"Stop before you start telling us about how a different style of parenting will prevent this kind of loss."

"Seriously, don't tell me I look strong or great or tired or good. Don't tell me I've lost weight and it suits me. Don't tell me your opinion about my looks!"

"When you want to say something but don't know what to say, don't use clichés like 'everything happens for a reason,' 'she's in a better place,' 'you should get back on that horse and move on'. Your clichés are meaningless to me."

Practicing sensitivity towards people who are grieving can help heal the sorrow. Insensitivity can exacerbate the pain.

Compassion will help repair feelings like:

- shock that won't end,

- sadness that hovers over everything,

- emptiness that appears at every family gathering,

- despair that returns at each family celebration or birthday.

This time of year is packed full of joyful reminders of the pain of loss. Graduation ceremonies can be brutal without a cheering father in the stands, a mother to fuss about details for a party, a child to walk across the stage with friends, or a BFF who always seemed like the "life of the party." Weddings, traditionally held during this time of year, also can be agonizing reminders of a future that will never happen and a past that ended too soon.

Most of us are not naturally attentive to the emotional journey of people who are grieving. As bystanders, we show up for funerals and send sweet condolences during the months that follow, but we move on quickly with our daily routines and lives. When loss can be kept at a distance, life can go on as if.....

For all these reasons, this time of year calls for a new level of sensitivity for the heartache of grief.

Consider, as an alternative to commenting on how someone looks, saying something like, "I am so glad to see you."

Rather than sending a traditional "JOY" card at holidays, send a personal note that simply says "love you."

Resist the temptation to suggest ways that people "should" be parents or caretakers of sick relatives. Being judgmental about anyone can precipitate unnecessary guilt and anger.

We are all, somewhat, cultural "bulls in china shops" when it comes to grief. None of us has the corner-stone for getting our words "right" every time. But being sensitive in the midst of joy and celebration is a worthy practice. Someday, any one of us could be standing in a room full of happiness after a huge loss and wish someone would recognize our loneliness and isolation.

In my first article for this column, I quoted Tom Ashbrook, the host of NPR's *On Point*. He had recently lost his wife and had just returned to work after a period of grieving. His program was titled "Grief and Comeback." He said, "One thing we know about life that is terrible and true: it ends. We don't get a choice about that. And sooner or later, that end comes to people that we love. And then, we grieve. In the past two months, that's been my path. A much-loved partner, lost. And plenty of grief. But for all the personal pain of it, grieving is an utterly universal experience. It comes to us all, essentially, at some point, over a parent, a lover, a friend, a child. It is one of the most human experiences. We are looking for some wisdom in this hour on how to make it through. And live again."

In the spirit of practicing sensitivity, may we be a kind and loving community whose aim is to encourage people to live again!

## From friends all over
## In Their Own Words

Hi Laura!

I was just reading your article in the newspaper this morning and was overwhelmed with gratitude that you are a member of our community. You have such a gift of compassion and an exceptional way of communicating that. Thank you for sharing your gifts!

Today you are in my heart and prayers for the comfort that you provide others. Much love.

*All the best,*
*Kelly Gray*

Dear Laura,

Thank you for your recent column "Goodbye: A hard but healing word."

If you remember in the many group meetings we had, I mentioned that my son never knew he was dying and always thought he would be going back to his home. It would have been too painful for him to know he was that ill, so I never said goodbye to him either. So whether a sudden death or a long, lingering one, goodbye is never easy. Again, Laura, thank you for all your columns. I may not comment on every one, but I find all of them very comforting.

*Rosemary Serino*

Dear Laura,

The piece you wrote for the newspaper about the private pain women experience was so beautiful, It touched me. What I would say to any woman stuck in pain and alone with it is to find a way to go into the experience. Don't push it away, sit with all of it, let the feeling come. Then forgive yourself, forgive everyone, and let your feelings take shape in some physical manner. Don't hold back, use whatever means you are comfortable with, for me it was art, maybe someone else would write, sing, chant , build. Do what feels natural make your own closure however you see fit. Then let hope and life enter in again. I don't know if this is helpful but your words opened my heart.

Thank you.

*Heidi Newfell*

Hello, Laura,

...I graduated from Salem State in 1971 and married my first and only love two weeks later. My husband and I met at Salem State. We had our three children very young and loved being married to each other. We both began our careers as teachers. Well, on Dec. 20, 2003, the Saturday before Christmas and 6 months before my second daughter's wedding. My husband went for a jog around the lake in Wakefield and collapsed and died.

There was nothing that could have been done. My blessing was that he had stopped into my shop before the run — never mentioning his plan to go, but he did give me a kiss goodbye. I was devastated, my children were devastated. We were brave as we tried to carry each other through the days and months that followed.

After reading the article you wrote about Paul McCartney's song "Let It Be," I knew I could reach out to you. I've read many of the articles you have written. They are wonderful. I admire the vocation you have chosen. Please continue to write and encourage people to look for the signs and the angels that come into our lives from day to day. It means so much to see our loved ones in a dream or hear a song on the radio at a very odd time, or those pennies you mentioned being found. Thank you.

*N.R.*

If grief were a garden overrun by weeds, Laura would be the garden consultant by your side saying, "Look. You will never get rid of all of the weeds, but you can learn to manage them. Yes, we can pull many right now, freeing the beautiful plants beneath, but, in time, more weeds will return. The good news is, by the time they do return, you will know what to do and your garden will continue to not only thrive, but grow." There are no words that can really express my gratitude for Laura's guidance; a "thank you" is just not good enough. With her guidance I have learned that life can grow and thrive amongst grief and that life, for me, is becoming much more beautiful than my previous one. If you are suffering from grief and heed her words, I promise that you will, in time and with lots of hard work, learn the same thing.

*Clark Webb*

"I want to talk to Laura." This realization hit me one day after six months of shepherding my 20-year-old son through his recovery from a traumatic brain injury resulting from a suicide attempt. He had jumped from his fourth floor college dorm window and was left completely and permanently blind.

We had been consumed by the day-to-day demands of nine days in an ICU, ten weeks in a rehab hospital, and several months of transition at home.

Laura helped me resolve a very difficult paradox. Laura helped me more fully articulate my grief, the sadness over the lost hopes and dreams for my family resulting from our irrevocably changed lives. At the same time, Laura also gently guided me toward an understanding that for better or worse, our lost hopes and dreams were for the future, and were ultimately, not real.

Your loss will be different. Your path to recovery will be different. Laura will accompany and guide you along that path.

*Tim Leahy*

# Acknowledgments

I want to thank my children Ydiahna, Leonel, and Asia for reading every article and helping me every step of the way. I am deeply appreciative for all those who have trusted me with their healing throughout this year. And my heartfelt gratitude goes out to Doug and Kristina Brendel for sharing their talents and skills as editor, artist, and photographer.

# About the Author

I am an ordained minister in the United Church of Christ. I graduated from Episcopal Divinity School in 1986. My first Call to Ministry was serving women in prison at MCI Framingham, a maximum security prison in Massachusetts. Teaching courses in economic development and family reintegration allowed me to encourage new pathways for women and their children. Through preaching in congregations around New England I became an advocate for the spiritual health and wellbeing of incarcerated women and their families. During this period of time, I worked closely on issues regarding domestic violence, drug and alcohol addiction, HIV, suicide, and community awareness of prisoners in Massachusetts.

In 1998, I was called to parish ministry. Serving congregations in Newburyport, Salem, Boxford, Andover, West Concord, and Weston, MA, I have enjoyed both settled and interim ministries. My commitment to creating and sustaining Open and Affirming congregations has been an important aspect of my ministry.

As a trained grief counselor and local minister, in 2009 I became the Spiritual Advisor to military families who were grieving suicide. Working with the staff of an organization called TAPS (Tragedy Assistance Project for Survivors), I continue to be committed to helping military families advance their spiritual health after a suicide. I also lead local support groups for suicide survivors in my community.

Currently, I am the Chaplain at Salem State University, leading one of the first embedded spiritual life programs at a state university in Massachusetts. Accompanying students and employees through some of the transformational movements on campuses, continues to be an awakening experience for me. College campuses are places where students are speaking up about social justice issues. This is an challenging and rewarding time to be listening to the voices of young men and women, many of whom have experienced a suicide in their communities or families.

In January 2015 I started writing monthly articles for a column in the local *Newburyport Daily News* newspaper titled "Grief and Comeback." These essays form the heart of this book.

*Rev. Laura Biddle*

# Index of Illustrations